The Moon

by
Jenny Tesar

First published in Great Britain by Heinemann Library
Halley Court, Jordan Hill, Oxford OX2 8EJ,
a division of Reed Educational & Professional Publishing Ltd

OXFORD   FLORENCE   PRAGUE   MADRID   ATHENS   MELBOURNE
AUCKLAND   KUALA LUMPUR   SINGAPORE   TOKYO   IBADAN
NAIROBI   KAMPALA   JOHANNESBURG   GABORONE
PORTSMOUTH NH (USA)   CHICAGO   MEXICO CITY   SAO PAULO

First published 1997

02 01 00 99 98
10 9 8 7 6 5 4 3 2 1

ISBN 0 431 01463 9

British Library Cataloguing in Publication Data

Tesar, Jenny
  The moon. – (Space observer)
  1. moon – Juvenile literature
  I. Title
  523.3

This book is also available in hardback (ISBN 0 431 01462 0)
Printed and bound in Malaysia by Times Offset (M) Sdn. Bhd.

Acknowledgments
The publishers would like to thank the following for permission to reproduce
photographs:

Pages 4–5: ©Galen Rowell/Peter Arnold, Inc.; pages 6, 7, 8, and 18: Gazelle Technologies,
Inc.; pages 9, 10–11: ©NASA/Peter Arnold, Inc.; page 12: ©Ted Clutter/Photo
Researchers, Inc.; page 13: ©Jeff Greenberg/MRP/Photo Researchers, Inc.; pages 14–15,
16: ©John Bova/Photo Researchers, Inc.; page 17: ©Francois Gohier/Photo Researchers,
Inc.; page 19: ©NASA/Science Source/Photo Researchers, Inc.; pages 20–21: ©Julian
Baum/Science Photo Library/Photo Researchers, Inc.; pages 22–23: PhotoDisc, Inc.

The publishers would like to thank Hutchison Library/Jeremy Horner for permission to
reproduce the cover photograph.

Every effort has been made to contact the copyright holders of any material reproduced
in this book. Any omissions will be rectified in subsequent printings if notice is given to
the publisher.

Contents

Some words are shown in bold, **like this**. You can find out what they mean by looking in the Glossary.

What is the Moon?

The Moon is a big round ball of rock. It is Earth's nearest neighbour. It is about 384,000 kilometres (km) from Earth. If you could drive to the Moon in a car, it would take 200 days to get there.

Earth travels around the Sun in a big oval or **orbit**. At the same time, the Moon travels around Earth in an oval.

How big is the Moon?

From Earth, the Moon looks as big as the Sun. But the Sun is about 400 times wider than the Moon. The Moon looks the same size because it is much closer to Earth.

From Earth, the Moon looks as big as the Sun

This picture shows Earth rising above the Moon's surface

The Moon is also smaller than Earth. Earth is about four times bigger than the Moon.

The Moon's surface

The Moon's surface has dark and bright areas. The dark areas are smooth and flat. They are **plains**. The bright areas are rough. They are mountains and **craters**.

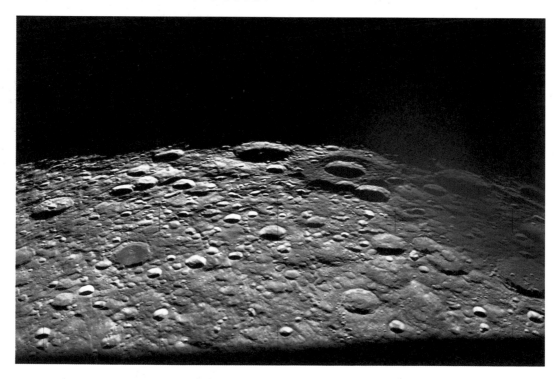

The Moon's surface has mountains and craters

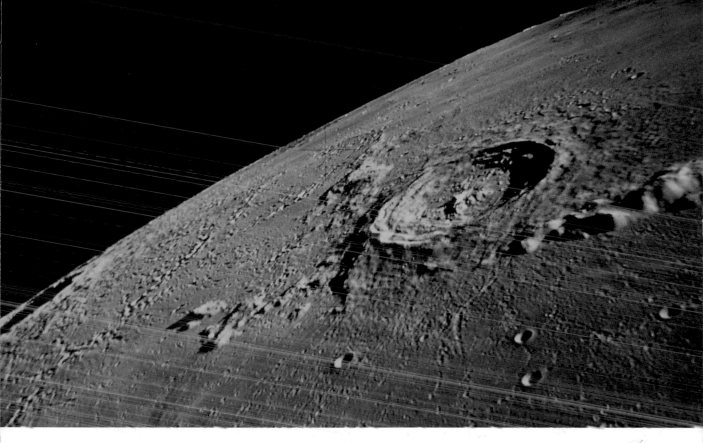

Craters look brighter than the smooth plains

Most of the Moon's craters were made by rocks flying through space. When the rocks crashed into the Moon, they made holes. The biggest one is so large it would take three hours to drive across it in a car!

The far side

The same side of the Moon always faces Earth. This is because the Moon doesn't spin as it travels around Earth. Most of us will never see the far side of the Moon.

Some spaceships carrying astronauts have circled the Moon. They took pictures of the far side. It looks a lot like the side that faces Earth.

The far side of the Moon

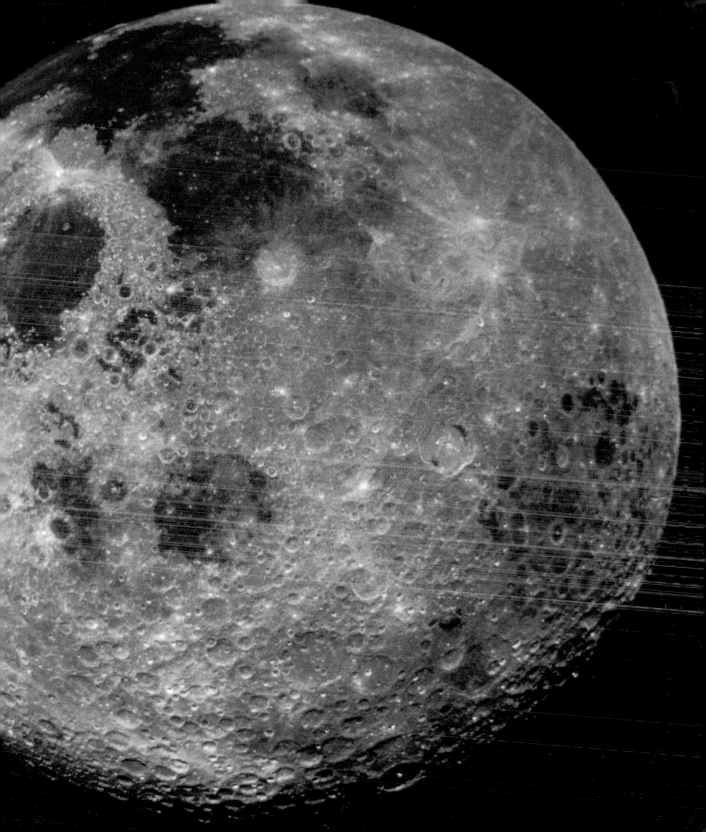

Tides

As the Moon travels around Earth it pulls on it. This pulling causes tides. When the Moon is over an ocean, the pull makes the water bulge. This is high tide.

When the Moon's pull on the ocean is strong, the tide is high

When the Moon's pull on the ocean is weak, the tide is low

As Earth spins, the ocean moves away from the Moon and the pull is less. The water level falls. This is low tide.

Phases of the Moon

The Moon's different shapes are called phases

The Moon does not make its own light. Sunlight hits the Moon and bounces off, or is reflected. The moon's **phases** are caused by the amount of sunlight that the moon reflects.

As the Moon moves around Earth, it looks as if it changes its shape. It shrinks from a full moon to a thin **crescent**. Then it seems to disappear. But soon the Moon is back, growing bigger again.

Eclipses

Sometimes, the Moon moves between Earth and the Sun. The Moon hides the Sun. This is called a solar (Sun) eclipse. The sky gets very dark, even though it is daytime.

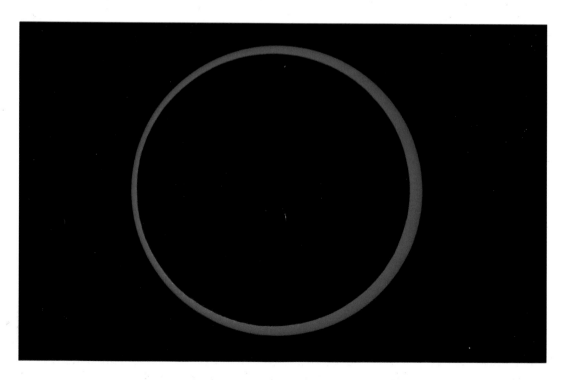

During a solar eclipse, the Moon hides the Sun

When the Moon is only partly eclipsed, only part of it is dark

Sometimes, Earth is between the Moon and the Sun. Then the Moon goes dark. This is a lunar (Moon) eclipse.

Never look right at the sun during an eclipse. The sunlight can hurt your eyes. It can even make you blind.

Visiting the Moon

For thousands of years, people could only look at the Moon from Earth. Then they built spaceships.

On 20 July 1969, two astronauts named Neil Armstrong and Buzz Aldrin stepped on the Moon.

Astronauts travel into space in rockets

Buzz Aldrin walks on the Moon

Armstrong and Aldrin were the first people ever to visit the Moon. In the years that followed, other astronauts also landed there.

Life on the Moon

There is no life on the Moon. The Moon has no air. It has little or no water. It is very hot on the side where it is lit by the sun. The dark side of the Moon is much colder than any place on Earth.

Someday, people may try to live on the Moon. They will have to bring air to breathe. They will also have to wear special clothes and eat special food.

Someday, people may live and work on the Moon at a base like this one

The Moon and everyday life

The Moon is important to people. Our word month comes from the word moon.

The Moon causes tides, which sometimes cause flooding during storms. The movement of the water from high tide to low and back also cleans the beaches. Around the world – near the oceans or thousands of kilometres away – the moon adds beauty to the night sky.

Glossary

craters Holes made by objects such as rocks.

crescent A shape that looks like a slice of melon.

orbit The path followed by the Moon.

phase Each different shape that the Moon appears to take.

plains Large areas of land that are very flat.

More Books to Read

Asimov, Isaac. *Why Does the Moon Change Shape?* Milwaukee, WI: Gareth Stevens, 1991.

Kelley, True. *What the Moon is Like.* New York: HarperCollins Children's Books, 1986.

Krupp, E. C. *The Moon and You.* New York: Simon & Schuster Childrens, 1993.

Rosen, Sidney. *Where Does the Moon Go?* Minneapolis, MN: Lerner Group, 1992.

Sullivan, George. *The Day We Walked on the Moon.* New York: Scholastic Inc., 1990.

Index